POE_____

presents

Bloom.

Poems of Loss, Heartbreak,

and New Beginnings.

Edited by R.J. Hendrickson

Bloom: Poems of Loss, Heartbreak, and New Beginnings.

Copyright © 2018 Ryan J. Hendrickson.

First Kindle Edition: October 2018

ISBN: 9781729189511

For permission requests or general inquiries, email the publisher at the following email address:
poemwarsoffical@gmail.com.

If you enjoyed this book, please leave an Amazon review and share it with others!

Cover Design by germancreative

R.J. Hendrickson Publishing
Boston, MA
www.poemwars.com

~

To Rachel,

who shone brighter

than the sun.

~

"It's so mysterious,

the land of tears."

- Antoine de Saint-Exupéry,

The Little Prince

CONTENTS

The Wind *cont'd*

Introduction

When I started putting together *Bloom*, I had no idea what I would be getting into. The initial goal was to convince nine or ten poets to submit a group of poems and then to combine them into a compilation, a collection of poetry addressing the themes of heartbreak, grief, and loss. It seemed simple enough.

The reason I had picked these particular themes was because they surrounded me at that time. Since I had moved back to Massachusetts, I witnessed an uncommon amount of death and loss. Suicide, overdoses, the passing of the sick and the elderly to something beyond - I witnessed grief, grief in its purest form, and broken hearts that refused to heal. More than anything, I witnessed people who didn't know how to cope with these tragedies, and it filled me with a frustrated sorrow, a feeling of empty helplessness.

How do people heal? How do we cope with losing those that we love, whether to death or to heartbreak? For me, the answer had always been in poetry. It was a personal therapy. Every word that I wrote, every sentence or stanza that made the page cleared a little weight from my soul and helped to clarify my sadness.

With this in mind, I formed *Poem Wars*, an online collective of poets who could share their work, and I immediately observed that many others dealt with their emotions in the same way that I did. As my community continued to grow, so did the depth and scope of this understanding: people needed an outlet to express their pain, otherwise it sat inside them and left them broken.

So, I decided to publish *Bloom* and try to address that pain, thinking that perhaps a few good poets with a few good poems could help at least a few people in pain who needed to realize that they weren't alone. Struggling to pick the right poets from such a large pool, I took myself out of the equation and opened submissions to my entire community.

The result was astounding.

In only three weeks, I received thousands of submissions. There were poems filled with hope and poems filled with despair. Some examined life, and others examined death. Some asked questions, and others answered them. It was clear - grief, loss, and heartbreak affect all of us. And, even more so, these are universally troubling experiences that people need to express, to let go and heal from.

Choosing the right poems for the book was extremely difficult and labor-intensive because so many of the poems deeply affected me. The words were unflinchingly personal. The poets poured their hearts out onto the page. Eventually I narrowed it down to the ones that I felt most closely addressed the theme and set out compiling, organizing, and editing. I convened with the poets to understand more about them - who they were, where they were from, and what they were getting themselves into with *Bloom*. Their responses were truly remarkable - their enthusiasm humbling and overwhelming.

In the end, I chose over 75 different poets from 25 different countries to participate, and each had a unique story to tell. To me, it was proof that this book needed to see the light of day.

In order to give the poems and themes more context, and to place them in the right order and flow, I've written a short parable, called *The Well*, that breaks up the book into six separate chapters. Each chapter addresses different aspects of the themes and how they affect us at our core. I hope the story helps to guide you on your journey through the words of these poets, words which changed me as I read them day after day.

I know they will change you too.

Without further ado, I present to you:
Bloom.

Best,

R.J. Hendrickson

POEM WARS

Bloom.

POEM WARS

<u>part one</u>

THE FALL

POEM WARS

~

T HE BOY woke up in a well.

He slowly lifted his head out of the tepid, muddy water which lay in a shallow pool at the bottom, surrounded by an echoing darkness.

The drought that had stretched for forty days had consumed most of the grasses in the fields and twisted them into a withering greyness, the land slowly drained of life under the scorching sun. The once full well had slowly emptied, day after day. Now the water lay only inches from the bottom, just enough to reach his nostrils and scraped cheeks caked in dirt and cause him to splutter awake.

Putting a hand on the wall, the boy leaned back, eyes squinting, taking in the sunlight high, high above, now a pinprick in the dark tunnel that surrounded him like a tomb.

"*Sana! Ramit!*" He yelled up to the ground far above him, but no one answered.

The walls were lined in a thick layer of slippery moss that broke under the trail of his fingertips, the stones worn and smoothed by centuries of rain. The boy wondered why the rain had stopped. Some of the elders said it was because the gods were angry at man, and that this year Spring would not come.

As he rose to his feet, a sharp pain coursed through his leg like a lightning bolt, causing him to gasp. His ankle looked bent and swollen, and blood pooled around the bottom of his sandals as it dripped down deep scrapes that ran along his leg. Breathing in deeply, he looked up again at the distant light, his voice too choked in fear to yell. The fear surrounded him, rising higher than the walls, thicker than the darkness.

One thought alone echoed through his head.

I am going to die.

Bloom.

I'm no longer
the man I used to be.
the night doesn't
speak to me anymore.

- sam baker | *flowers and thorns*

Nigeria
https://www.instagram.com/sammbakery/

Why did I let you slip through my fingertips
Like sand
I wanted to hold you for longer
Than an hourglass
I wanted to stare into your eyes
As though they were clouds and I was making
shapes.
I'm in bad shape
Like trees in winter

- zach whitman | *shapes*

New York City, New York
https://www.instagram.com/zachwhitmanlive/

Bloom.

August heat
drive them home
the red convertible
the hot sun on her face
the eager and hopeful child
oh that sun
the joy of running back
into the arms that kept her safe
gave her strength
the wild horses racing along the highway
their beauty so wild so free
could it be real
familiar street
Long Island sweet
cars up and down endlessly
home yes home
honeysuckle Lilac yard
find her
the sobs of crying neighbors
the silent faces
why
fear
dread
find her
she is there
find her
calling her
she is there
find her
every room

cont'd

calling her
find her
is she there
find her
is she here
find her
can't find her
the father kneels
tender are his words
to his little girl with fear in her eyes
no embrace
no goodbye
she is gone
take me
God take me to her
she is gone
as is the child in her

- meg de laura | *ida's girl*

Long Island, New York
https://www.instagram.com/redsgrl3/

Bloom.

Switched through countless drugs
Ended up hooked on you
I can't precisely ever
Choose what was worse
The curse that threw you
In my way of addictions
Or the hangover that followed
Causing my very extinction

- karan sharma |
my worst addiction

Punjab, India
https://www.instagram.com/zationar_official/

POEM WARS

The water was clear
The waves rippled gently
The sand was soft
And the sun was beaming hot

You were glowing
Your eyes, gleaming
And my cheeks were rosy pink
My lips, luscious red from your
constant kissing
My skin, softer than a baby's butt
And your smell, lingered on me for days
to come

But now,
The water is salty
The sand is rough
The sun is scorching
And my skin, dull

The waves, crashing down on my face

- a.m.j. | *today i am drowning*

Los Angeles, California
https://www.instagram.com/my_unspoken_art/

16

Bloom.

His heart gripped
In shaking fingertips
A clench, a twist
Into a hard fist
The throbbing palm
Now stained in red pain
Then paints the face
Of his broken remains

- arden grey | *loving hurts*

USA
https://www.instagram.com/darkwriterssociety/

you laughed
        and felt like a stranger.

    life has hurt too long.

- brian | *you laughed*

San Diego, California
https://www.instagram.com/writtendragonfly/

Bloom.

Tragic, fearful, hating creature
Breathing even though I shouldn't
Living here without a purpose
Hiding from the guarding angels
Can't find the strength to fight the shadows
Crawling out at night and I can't
Seem to find the missing piece I'm
Hurting everything that's good.

How dare you try to reach me now when
I'm cleaning up the mess they made
They left me here without a reason
I will only make you sorry
I can't forgive your glory when I'm
Walking over broken mirrors
Don't ever try to wake me up again
I'd rather let the memories choke me

Tragic, fearful, fragile creature
I am just a parasite
Blowing out your candle
Killing all the lights.

- tiger s. | *parasite*

Trollhattan, Sweden
https://www.instagram.com/mindoftigersweettooth/

You're all the colors
in the sky.
but
even sunsets go out
with a big bang
before leaving you
in the dark

- dez | *big bang*

Los Angeles, California
https://www.instagram.com/phil0phobiv/

Bloom.

I don't know what changed between us.
Sentences are replaced by words.
Calls into silence.
My inbox is full but not a single message
from you.
Long morning calls
are just good morning texts.
Weekly meetings changed to monthly,
and monthly to yearly.
24/7 became
24 seconds.

Ignorance hurts
I know
but silence in conversation
haunts
more.

- shruti | *silence haunts*

The trees grew fast over the past
few years.
Side by side, tight and defensive
reliably kept out of the familiarity of grief

It took one glance and one smile
and with a few seconds
you cut off all the roots.

- an.na | *defenseless*

Berlin, Germany
https://www.instagram.com/an.na.poetry/

Bloom.

In a flash, you were gone.
Unwilling to go further,
Unwilling to murmur, why, truly.

Tales of "this is for your good."
If only you did it sooner,
Than stir emotions
You would not tend,
Cast a future,
Only to end
It abruptly with no care,
Dismantle a dream
I once held dear.

- camille a. frazer | *heartbroken*

Hanover, Jamaica
https://www.instagram.com/camilleamar_legacycreator/

POEM WARS

We used to count the stars
On a cloudy night
We used to create infinities
Every time our bodies would collide
And our souls locked in embrace
We used to dance barefoot in the rain
Living up to clichés
Of lovers
Who will always remain

Which is why, my love
The blood seeping out of my fingers
Is insignificant a price to pay
As I tear apart your grave
And join you in bed
The last thing I see
Before the earth falls back in place
Is a smile forming where your mouth
Might have been, had any flesh
Been covering your face

- zainab | *sane insanity*

Islamabad, Pakistan
https://www.instagram.com/capturing_words_/

24

Bloom.

I pumped my veins with dose
after dose of cocktails
of prescriptions
I swallowed handfuls of
little blue capsules
Dark as your eyes
Until my vision was cloudy again
Numb to every emotion
I slept until
the sun went down and came back up again
Slowly, as if urging me to wake
My throat stung
And my hands shook
But I could
finally not hear your laugh
Echoing in my head

- meg | *your laugh*

Ocean City, Maryland
https://www.instagram.com/poetrybymeg/

Your light attracted my shadows
too heavily
it stretched them out so far
that they couldn't be seen within
your luminescence
but the night always comes my dear
and i can't help that

- bernad hasanovic |
illuminated curtains

Atlanta, Georgia
https://www.instagram.com/dankenhein/

Bloom.

she ran from
a love that
ignited her soul
tripped & swiftly
fell into a well
filled with
nothing to
drown in

- alex bingham |
the other side

Union, New Jersey
https://www.instagram.com/thealexbingham/

27

POEM WARS

Bloom.

part two

THE MOTH

POEM WARS

Bloom.

~

THE BOY'S breathing began to steady, and his eyes adjusted to the darkness. The well's silence was accompanied by a steady *drip drip,* water leaking from deep beneath the earth through the various cracks in the stone, sliding down the moss like tiny waterfalls.

Mud soaked his sandals and pushed its way between his toes, pulling him deeper into the shallow pool. The boy leaned over and took a small handful of water, which rested clear and calm above the soaked earth. He sipped it and it drifted down his throat, cool and fresh, quenching his thirst and emptying his head of thoughts. The sip was the first clean water he had tasted in weeks.

As he leaned down for another handful, there was a sudden flutter of movement beneath the surface, causing the boy to jump back. Pain shot through his leg, vibrating in his bones. He peered down at the mud. Poking through the surface of the water was a large moth, its burnt-orange wings heavy with the thick mud. The boy picked it up, holding the moth gingerly in his outstretched hand. It writhed and struggled as it shook dirt and water from its wings. Slowly the moth began to calm, perhaps sensing the presence of its young protector, now freed from the grasp of the drowning earth.

The boy wiped its wings with his wet fingers, cleaning off the mud, and - with a sudden flutter - the moth stood tall in the center of his palm, wings outstretched and ready for a rapid getaway. The boy stared deep into the its primitive, unblinking eyes, a fellow soul captive in the depths of this prison womb. There wasn't fear in those dark, unblinking eyes. There wasn't hope or courage or anger or despair. There was only the impulse to survive, to drift away from danger to something better, to attempt an escape from the smothering darkness. Far, far above was a place with light to warm its back and air to lift its wings and an unshakeable freedom.

They stood there together in the mud, the boy blind and shivering in the echoing silence, the moth perched quietly in his hand. He took a deep breath and looked up.

Far above, there was light, and he could hear the wind.

Bloom.

Drifting through the darkening halls
from room to room
shadows grow
gliding across the walls
the silence loud and
crackling
he wonders on his life
loves
dust dancing through beams
we know nothing of time,
we know nothing of death
we are here until we are not
alone
ageless in those moments
timeless
he remembers the boy in those moments
sees through his eyes
a familiar melancholy washes over him
warm
soft
insistent
he thinks loss is all there is
as it turns out

- brett curley | *drifting through the darkening halls*

Boston, Massachusetts
https://currentrant.wordpress.com/

sad

my wildest dreams
were once my reality

where'd you go, my love?

- mrssi | *solitude*

Orange County, California
https://www.instagram.com/sincerelymrssi/

Bloom.

Sometimes I am warm
like sand and
sometimes I am blue as the sea

Mostly I am deep as the ocean
and you came to discover
me

But there is no grace
jumping into the waves
of a love you don't
intend to keep
Still, you jumped in knowing
you would drown
you jumped in knowing
it was too deep

- vicky frissen | *swim*

Netherlands
https://www.instagram.com/dancinginthemoonlines/

They fell in love,
But the universe mourned,
For they were two parallel lines.
Always side by side
But could never coincide.

- janhvi gupt | *collateral love*

Stavanger, Norway
https://www.instagram.com/picturesque_passion/

Bloom.

Mind: I want to run away.

Heart: Why would you want to?

Soul: Because when she wakes up
in the middle of the night,
I feel lonely.

- maria feliza inez | *three people*

Rotorua, New Zealand
https://www.instagram.com/metamarfisis/

For the first time, I woke
up under a roof of misery
windows are open
but no sight of glee
the chirpy birds are quiet
maybe they soared to a
place where it's sunny
I envy them.

Summers didn't
bring sun for me.
You seem to have woken
up pretty early,
left without the morning routine.
My head hurts
I can't remember
a thing
Just that we drifted off
on love songs

No wonder why
it's still asleep.

- priya tomar | *morning*

Madhya Pradesh, India
https://www.instagram.com/much_philosophy/

Bloom.

My heart no longer sobs
when I hear your name

- megan ledger | *a lie*

Wallington, United Kingdom
https://www.instagram.com/meganlledger_/

The moon kisses
the ocean
like you used to
kiss me

Cloaked
in clandestine desire

Our love
disappears
with the tide

- caleigh morgan | *tide*

New Hampshire, USA
https://www.instagram.com/crystalmermaid_poetry/

Upon the realization
that I was merely a string
for you to pull along

- k.l.n. | *strung*

Auckland, New Zealand
https://www.instagram.com/kl.newms/

Wisping smoke dances from my shattered nerves.

I sit alone in blackness & silence.

As if the stone rolled from the tomb
Has lodged in the doorway of my room.

And every time I rise, I am reminded
of the fact
That three days have passed & she
still has not come back.

- ian curtin | *the empty tomb*

Cork, Ireland
https://www.instagram.com/elcurtino/

42

Bloom.

i never got to hold you
i never got to see you
i never got to touch you
all i have is
a date to remember you by
and the love i never got to give you

- kay | *too perfect for earth*

Charlotte, North Carolina
https://www.instagram.com/with.love.kay/

If they tell me of a river
that I could swim
to get back to you
I'd go by it
along with buckets
to empty it
wasting the rest of my life
to put an end to that river.
So that by no chance
and by no mistake
I could swim back to you

So that by no chance
I get back to you.

- li | *never back to you*

New Delhi, India
https://www.instagram.com/justhowliwrites/

Bloom.

I wondered if it is the
wetness that comes from
the water touching the
soil,
Or if it is the endless
raindrops running down
the window,
That makes me reminisce,
The times when we kissed,
And the tears you had
running down my face,
I wish it wasn't over,
But we were like the
rain,
Cold and drenched in our
pain.

- hemah kris | *we were like the rain*

Malaysia
https://www.instagram.com/wordsnevergounwritten/

45

under the night defined by milky ways
the wild ferns of my yearning grew

I was waiting to write the story of us
with words that will never reach you

- d. neil | *it will never reach you*

India
https://www.instagram.com/neilscape/

Bloom.

.

Never drown yourself in
the same river twice.

- simra sadaf | *drown yourself*

India
https://www.instagram.com/balladoflife/

POEM WARS

Where did you go?
I saw the blue roses
begin to weep and wilt
this frosted morning,
and azure skies
closing over grey,

something left today
and the world looked
quite the same
to all but me,
I felt an absence
between my heartbeats
I heard a mournful echo
between the stop and start
of the breeze,
and a laughter breaking
down, slumping low
into muffled tears.

He told me everything
is waiting for me
but that's not what I've seen.

Maybe everything
will be beautiful again
tomorrow.

- siomar ballan | *blue roses wilting*

London, United Kingdom
https://www.instagram.com/poet.sulee/

<u>part three</u>

THE CLIMB

POEM WARS

Bloom.

~

HIS FINGERS grasped at the rocks, searching for cracks and edges, combing through the moss and lichens. He lifted a sandal, pressing his foot firmly against the lip of the protruding stone. It slipped and fell back into the squelching mud. The boy removed his sandals, ignoring the dull ache of his ankle as the moth fluttered near his head, watching over him, testing its wings in the cold, damp air. His feet now bare, he recovered his grip, toes balanced in the wall's cracks, small fingers wedged safely in the smooth crevices.

The boy began to climb.

Slowly, step by step, grasp by grasp. He let his breath out in short gasps, intaking sharply with every new handgrip and upward swing. He thought about the drought and the gods and if Spring would come. He thought about the elders and their stories and the rain. The moth hovered close by, loyal, unwilling to leave its tired companion among the dripping walls and the wailing of the winds.

He climbed and climbed, higher and higher and higher, and the opening of the well brightened like the morning sun, burning across his upward horizon. The stones slipped with moss and the damp trickle of water that leaked through its cracks, hidden deep in the earth, far below the deadened surface scorched by merciless weeks of unrelenting heat. But his small fingers held, fitting into the small grooves of rock, tightening around vines and clumps of crumbling clay.

As he climbed he imagined the stars, the mountains at morning, Sana's smile as she hid her eyes behind her thick black hair. The savory aroma of *bhaji* drifting through the house, his mother at the stove, his father settled contemplative at the table, dusty sandals by the door. He saw the river as it took him and Ramit on their backs through green *badam* trees, past wriggling golden *mahseer* and the shade of the Himalayas cutting across the afternoon.

The moth floated above him among the red dust that soon drifted through the air as the wind swelled above. It floated higher and higher until it glimmered at the top, alight in a sunbeam, before it was hit by a gust of wind and swept off along with the swirl of the red dust. The boy reached higher, when his hand grasped a handful of dirt. His feet suddenly slid downward as dust whipped through the air and he fumbled for a new grip on the stone. His fingers frantically slipped between a crack and he steadied. He peered up, tightening his grip on the wall. The top of the well was caved in, the edge sloping downward as the earth crumbled and funneled into the vanishing bottom. He looked across. The stone ran smoothly up to the well's top edge, solid and even, but to either side of that escape was slippery moss, creeping across his path, blocking his way around, mocking him.

He turned to the center of the well and looked up.

A lone rope dangled and swayed with the wind, swinging an old wooden bucket in a pendulum arc just feet from his head. Both of his hands gripped the wall tightly, fear gripping him even tighter. He could not reach out with one hand without risking a steep fall all the way back down to the muddy bottom.

He would have to leap.

The boy thought of the aroma of *bhaji* and the mountain shadows and Ramit in the river and Sana's smile and he leapt, feet pushing hard off of the wall, hands stretched out into the void.

For a moment he floated, alone in the darkness, suspended in the sunbeam, a lonely moth fluttering in the swirling dust. There was no well and no wall and no drought. There was just an empty and exhilarating nothingness, a freedom past the pain in his ankle and the beating of the sun. There was only silence, a pulsing, endless silence.

His hand grasped the rope, and he swung in a smooth arc, quickly pulling his feet atop the bucket. He hugged the rope tightly and the swinging slowed until he hung, still, suspended in the air. The boy looked down below his feet. The bottom of the well was gone, buried in the dark. Turning his head to the sky, the boy measured the remaining length of rope with his eyes. It was less than the length of his body.

Grasping the rope hard, he began to pull himself up.

The wood snapped.

He was falling, the walls rushing around him in a blur, the light above disappearing from his reach as he was swallowed up in the void. The rope hit its end. All of his force came to a sudden halt, pulling his hands rapidly along the length of the rope as his feet slipped from the bucket. Another *snap*. The rope turned to a wriggling serpent in his hands, uncoiling as he fell to the muddy earth, welcoming him back into its void.

Bloom.

Her silence was taken for granted,
Her worst nightmare became her reality,
Her strength became her weakness,
Her pure soul, drenched with fear,
As her life became a target
A target foreign to her.

Her voice drowned with the sound of the spectators
watching and applauding.
Her desperate cry for help was turned on to deaf ears,
Her pain still echoed in the dead of the night.

- simmie d. | *the dead of night*

Mumbai, India
https://www.instagram.com/simmie_d_talks/

This is rage.
And it's the sting of an angry wasp-
The lash of a grinning whip.
The progression of your tongue
Is the recession of my steps.
Dust.

Yes dear, it's collecting.

- narcissa lyons | *noise*

New York, USA
https://www.instagram.com/narcissa_lyons/

Bloom.

I'm a white rose,
with a black shadow.
I'm the moon
With the black mark.
I'm the poetry
With painful words.
I'm the sky,
full of scars.
My heart is filled with love while my mind
is haunting me.
My soul is a galaxy which feels empty in space.

- smea | *mixed blessing*

Hyderabad, India
https://www.instagram.com/prathyusha_sameera/

POEM WARS

There are certain things you want to remember

There will be people that will tell you to keep
dreaming
But will do things to turn the same into ember.
They'll tell you how your strength has no boundaries
and to keep believing.
But their dreams and yours
They will dismember.
Show you how the grass is greener on their side.

There will be certain things they won't tell you
About weeds that don't belong
And unbloomed flowers that died
And for once, you might even believe them,
That your garden isn't worth its gems,
That all the time you've spent on it is worthless
That dreams aren't ageless.

But they'll tell you to keep dreaming
Dreams that require leaving behind
Your side screaming
To be dreamt about again.
To not be left to drain.

cont'd

Bloom.

It's up to you to hear their plea
Or to let them be
To let them be forgotten until the other side
Becomes a forest you get lost in
Trying to put out the forest fire and the siren
Looking for a way home,
Only to find it barren.

- juhi | *of dreams and reality*

India
https://www.instagram.com/jfipoetry/

We both are
just two souls,
walking barefoot on fire
but you don't care
if you're burning
all you crave for
is to watch both of us
evaporate,
rise up
and fall down as
tears from our eyes.

- aaradhya | *rain on fire*

Ghaziabad, India
https://www.instagram.com/aaradhya04/

Bloom.

you were my favorite heartbreak.

- christian vincent champe |
favorite heartbreak

Las Vegas, Nevada
https://www.instagram.com/mrgrey_poetry/

o, helios, as you set and
pass out of sight
watch over my beloved
in her far off country

make her day gay and bright,
cast your rays on her pious body;
a sermon of warm evocations

selene, is that you drifting
into view
did you do as promised and
whisper sweet lamentations

did she stir, or murmur at all
bathe her room in sweet melancholia
with the wish for a better future

it will be the day of all days
when I look up to you from that window
but alas, not today
and now goodnight

- jack goodwright | *with erebos*

London, England
https://www.instagram.com/wandering__albatross/

Bloom.

Fourteen times the clock struck midnight before I
realized that the blue of the paint has been chipped.
The tea cup that you painted is still sitting in the
cupboard.
The suit that you rented is thrown over the bedroom
chair.
But most of all the note that you left in my purple
notebook with golden edges still says,

"I will be back soon."

- rebecca fran | *the final note*

Guyana, South America
https://www.instagram.com/rebeccafranwrites/

For me her hands were bath time,
bubbles and bubbles and bubbles.
she'd build me castles of pristine white while
a melody of a rubber ducky danced
from her lips across the soapy surface,
leaving footprints in the foam.

the wrinkles at the corners of her mouth
framed a laugh that was breathless and shimmering.
the one we knew then
has long gone but that sing-song voice remains,
haunting her being
like a home abandoned,
bouncing off walls, falling
down steps that groan,
bones broken banisters,
skin chipping paint,
a reminder of something once beautiful.

her thoughts drift softly like
dust in the dawn that
creeps through curtains,
no purpose, no presence.

cont'd

Bloom.

her sentences are scattered,
pages ripped from novels and
shoved back out of order
yellowed and smelling of lives lived and laid in ink,
left on the wooden floor for the wind to walk with.

the sheet with my name has vanished,
and she'll never know it
or me again.

- g. konstantin | *atrophy*

Somerville, Massachusetts
https://www.instagram.com/gracekay_/

POEM WARS

He promises roses
But he has no way of growing them
Stems, petals, roots
Thorns,
Rose bushes.

Superficial;
He knows only the hues,
the tints of reds, perhaps
He'll waste most of your time on
Yellows, remorse for his inconvenience
For relieving your flesh of thorns.

He promises roses,
And that's exactly what you will get.
Plucked from life, he gifts them
Plucked from truth he'll lie-
In your arms.

You and the roses are the same.
Waiting for your love to wither in vain,
In the depths of a shallow hand
that never dared to know
the soil.

- kereen lotus | *he promises roses*

Queens, New York
https://www.instagram.com/lotus_ker/

Bloom.

A man once told me to never chase the
butterflies and I never knew what it
meant until our love turned to
gray and my heart was desperate for you
to call my name.

- britney terrazas | *never chase the butterflies*

El Monte, California
https://www.instagram.com/b.v.writing/

Looking in a mirror,
I found a girl.
Same height as me,
Same body,
Same physique.

She's painted with gray.
Grief was written on her face.
Scars covered her body,
Scars as fresh as an apple
And the marks that grew dry
On her gentle skin.

Her eyes were filled with tears and sorrow.
Covering the image of a girl
Wanting to escape and hide.
An image of me in her eyes.

The girl was me.
Imprisoned in someone's body.
Someone with an empty soul
and ripped edges.

Someone who doesn't know
How to smile
And someone who forgot
The word happiness.

cont'd

Bloom.

Everything is now clear.
All the searchings were for nothing.
It wasn't far,
The thing I had sought.
Because it was always here.

Everything is now clear.
I didn't lose myself somewhere.
Because
I lost myself in me.

- desiree | *lost and found*

Philippines
https://www.instagram.com/introvert_psycho/

She was just like a flower

She continued spreading fragrance
even when torn apart.

- ashis | *like a flower*

Mumbai, India
https://www.instagram.com/ashispoetry/

Bloom.

I wrote about the world
How it tricks and tempts us
And I wrote about its people
How they keep stumbling onto themselves
•

I wrote about the rain
How it washes away fear and regret
And I wrote about the drought that follows
How it breaks even the hardest of us.
•

I wrote about nature
Its beauty all encompassing
And I wrote about life
Its finiteness, the best teacher.
•

But ever since our paths crossed
All I ever wrote about
was you.

- burhan kutub | *i wrote about the world*

Pune, India
https://www.instagram.com/the.writester/

The night sky
It is as beautiful
as you
"The stars are dead"
So you said

You are twice as beautiful
when you die.

- ray | *beauty is death*

Kuwait
https://www.instagram.com/poeticfvck/

Bloom.

Sit.

Listen to the crackling fire, watch the embers rise into the night sky, witness our lives flash before our eyes while we sit here pretending everything is fine

Once, long ago, your words were heartfelt, your words felt real, your words held no lies

But they were only as real as you were and you vanished before I could tell you

You were my north star, my way back home, my truest friend

I cling to what used to be until my hands are bloodied and brittle. Have I lost you for good?

I thought we'd protect each other

I thought we'd walk through these woods hand in hand

But you've left me here to watch you stumble in the dark

I tried to warn you but you told me I didn't know what I was talking about

You only listen to the whispers that crawl up your veins, the smoke that leaves your eyes strained and bloodshot

You drink on, hoping the liquid courage will fight your demons for you, throwing empty bottles at your own reflection

cont'd

How cruel

You've let me stand here and watch while I lose you

Puff by puff, you disappear into the mist, into the night

I cry your name until it's unrecognizable on my tongue,
I've lost count of how many times my shirt was stained
with tears that fell for you, of how many times I've let
you back in despite the tired protest of my mind

But you're six-foot under and I can't reach you without
filling my lungs with the same poison

Why does letting go hurt deeper than the splintering in
my chest

I unravel my hands from yours, everything is dark and
desolate but now there's room for light

- hayat y. | *sore beginnings*

Adiss Ababa, Ethiopia
https://www.instagram.com/highvibeee/

part four

THE FLOWER

POEM WARS

~

Darkness.

Mud seeped into the boy's eyes, burning, blurring his vision as he coughed out muddy water in a choking splutter. The walls rumbled a deep echo toward the surface as he lay there, arms outstretched, the bucket beside him broken to pieces. Blood seeped from his palms, streaming down his arms and soaking into the mud below. The moth was nowhere to be seen.

He was alone.

The boy lay his head back into the pool, water filling his ears with muffled silence. He lay there in the mud, as time passed and the wind blew far above. He thought about the drought and the gods and if Spring would come. He thought about the elders and their stories and the rain. The boy wondered what would happen if it never rained again, and the thought made him sad, sadder than he had ever been.

He closed his eyes.

Then, from the silence came a sound, soft but clear. It beat and pulsed, the rhythm of a heart, the quaking of a mother's breath. Eyes closed, head pressed to the swelling earth, he heard the hum of a quiet, echoing song, not the gods or the rain or the elder's stories, but of something beyond fear. Something beyond death. Something beyond the withering grass.

The boy opened his eyes, and that's when he saw it. There, deep in the mud, was a flower.

Caught in a fragile sunbeam, it poked its head from the humming earth, reaching toward the sky, seeking the slowly vanishing light. Its petals were a vibrant purple, blooming outward from its brilliant, yellow heart of pollinated tendrils.

The boy breathed. Air filled his lungs. Water dripped from his face as he rose from the mud. He stood, staring at the sky overhead, taking in the darkness and the echoing song and the hum of the earth.

Far, far above, he could see the light and hear the whistling of the wind, and he suddenly forgot that he was afraid.

Bloom.

When pain asks me to dance
It is not a question.

She commands my quick-step-stumbles,
In a tawdry tango,
An unwieldy waltz.

We are a garish spectacle
As we wallow in the relentless rhythm of day,
And the monotonous melody of night.

She is a persistent partner, you see.
And I cannot refuse an old friend.

- ellen moynihan | *old friend*

Brisbane, Australia
https://www.instagram.com/odetocadence/

I dreamed
I held you again,
I kissed the whole of your
broken face.
But then I awoke,
and all your colors
turned to grey
ashes
that rest in the box on top
of my bedroom dresser.
And I wonder if I return you
to the earth,
will you return to me,
like the leaves that die
and fall
and come Spring, are born again?

- kristina boothe | *ashes*

Jacksonville, Florida
https://www.instagram.com/kristinaboothe/

Bloom.

Swing by sunset corner sometime
Nothing's changed, it remains the same
The driveway is lined with French Marigolds
Wild roses, even now, climb the cottage walls
Like robust rebels, defiant and uncontrolled;

You know it well, that sweet lime smell
How it grabs ahold of you and never lets you go.

Pass by won't you?
We'll sip on Boulevardier cocktails like we used to;
Liquid and potent, chaos and loss on the rocks,
Maybe tap our feet to our music past, bare in socks
We can get drunk on those bygone tales,
Tumble over waves of memories gone pale;
Of good ol' days, sweet love and heartache
We'll flip through the pages until daybreak
To a time of yellow bliss,
when our souls kissed.

- soli | *echoes of yellow*

St. Joseph, Trinidad and Tobago
https://www.instagram.com/soli.words/

You were like a drug.
A sentinel gently taking me by the hand
Guiding me into a dream world
Where the terrain was unfamiliar and
Unanticipated.

All those years together we fused into one being
Like a tree growing around a long
Forgotten headstone.

Without your tightly coiled vines I have finally
Made sense of the name carved here so close to
Me.

- kylee noel | *epitaph*

Thunder Bay, Canada
https://www.instagram.com/k_n_writes_/

Bloom.

I'm sorry baby
but my pride won't let me
put my cigarette down
I know that you're concerned
but I've got a whole lot of things
I've got to burn

- mr. lights | *burn*

South Gates, California
https://www.instagram.com/mr.lights/

POEM WARS

I tried fitting in this crowd,
as you said
that's how I would never feel lonely
you claimed.

I tried venting my heart out
that's how you said
We connect and reach out.

I tried loving everyone around
As you told me
the lost ones are found.

I tried wearing high heels
to look more appealing
that's how you told me
I would find myself some company.
But
It was strange how the
crowd made me feel lonelier.
I kept dreaming about nights
I spent on my terrace, counting stars,
and it made me feel so much better.

It's strange how my heart
felt heavy each time I vented
out to these people around.
I would rather be lost
in mountains,
never to be found.

cont'd

Bloom.

It's strange how loving
everyone around
fetched me nothing.
No wonder I found my
ripped sneakers more comforting.

Yes, I'm alone all the time
but never feel lonely.
Maybe because, unlike you,
I knew how to enjoy my own company.

- itti | *my own world*

Sardarshahar, India

Many years down the line
I still struggle to find myself.
Remind me in the next life to come
Never to give my soul
To someone who isn't whole.

- coOva | *wholesome love*

Lagos, Nigeria
https://www.instagram.com/travelwithcoova/

Bloom.

On the right I'm pastel pink,
lilac, white,
wrapped up in your arms. Your fingers
stuck
in my uncombed hair. My gaze
fixed
on your wandering eye. Our bodies
glued
to the unmade bed.

Time passes, nonetheless.
Contentment.

On the left an open window -
you feel the gentle breeze
against your blind back
and it dances
a short,
sweet dance, kisses you, and
leaves.

Time passes, nonetheless.
Contentment.

I see the window past you but
the breeze misses me. Your touch
paralyses.
On the right I'm overcome with red,
crimson, black.

cont'd

A void, constructed of my thoughts,
insecurities,
failings,
forces us apart.
I stare
envious of your seeming bliss.

Time passes, nonetheless.

At the start a door. The deepest blue.
You said you'd never leave
but in the morning you were gone.
My colours drowned you.

I pray you were saved.

- hannah hartley | *contentment*

England
https://www.instagram.com/hannahhartleyxo/

Bloom.

Taking a leap of faith off a cliff
Counting the layers of sediment
While I wait for these wings to catch air.

- johnny valdez | *wind*

Medford, Massachusetts
https://www.instagram.com/johnny_on_the_spot87/

POEM WARS

He looked at me and smiled
Saying that I reminded him
Of a Bob Dylan classic
Always wavering between
Where I was
Where I had been
And where I longed to be
A wandering daydreamer
With a vibrant love for love
Restlessly seeking the
Seemingly unattainable
Lost in a maddening state
Of indecisiveness

"How does it feel,"
He softly asked,
"To have no direction home,
Completely unrestrained by
The cities and their people?"
Well, it feels like freedom
But freedom only exists
When you have nothing to lose
And I'll tell you a secret…
Sometimes I waver with that too.

- chelsie collier | *like a rolling stone*

Ocala, Florida
https://www.instagram.com/c.collierpoetry/

90

Bloom.

Kind soul
All alone in a
Lonely world
Engrossed in confusion
In circles that twirl I'm
Damned to be happy
On my own

- kaleido | *self*

Johannesburg, South Africa
https://www.instagram.com/kaleido_peace/

I exiled myself to Paradise,
a defector from the East Coast hamster wheel,
accelerating at an ungodly pace,
fueled by Starbucks.
The rich azure hues of the seas
with their whispering breezes
echoed my name,
with majestic Ko'olau mountains blanketed in green,
tugging at my heart,
promising a peaceful transition of calm.
I desperately desired a serene and placid overhaul,
a reincarnation of the unsuspecting girl from my 20's
who exuded a happy, curious, wonderment.
She had no idea of the upcoming forces that would play
on her personality.

I became my father
critical of myself
critical of others,
with an acerbic wit and gallows humor
offending and affronting.
Though I traveled the world
with a coterie of friends,
I became a lesser version of myself.
My one bright light
My motherhood.
I adored my two sons
our many adventures together.
Yet, something was missing
and I needed to secure it.

cont'd

Bloom.

I thought living in the happiest place on Earth
would find it.
Never feeling the cold creep in
with the ever-present soleil.
Hiking through bamboo forests
to hidden waterfalls,
swimming, canoeing,
communing with the tides
exploring
reinventing
living with aloha
living with myself.

Here, the happiest place on Earth
Transient military friends
snowbirds
constantly saying good-bye,
7-day work weeks
Dumb-ass da kine
family phone-tag six hours behind
crazy yule-time plane rides
to catch a glimpse of my boys,
and still no sign of the girl from my past.

So, I returned.
The rich azure hues of the seas
With their whispering breezes
No longer echoed my name,
Majestic Ko'olau mountains blanketed in green
No longer tugging at my heart,
And suddenly I was calm.

cont'd

POEM WARS

I re-invented the wheel, one long forgotten
In a seaside village that had sheltered me
Almost 40 years ago.
I had forgotten its rocky beauty
its shoreline that tempted me to explore
its mysterious inlets
surrounded by darker,
richer tones,
its comforting history
and ever-evolving colors.
my light now bright again,
my sons no longer on a distant shore.

The young girl, nearly forgotten
Was leading me by the hand,
Leading me to the life
I had yet to remember,
I had yet to imagine,
I had yet to live.

- karen beth | *exile*

Kaneohe, Hawaii

94

Bloom.

As patience
And hope
Abandoned me
Time whispered

"I will keep you company."

- lola blue | *on a lighter note*

Sarajevo, Bosnia and Herzegovina
https://www.instagram.com/lolabluepoetry/

I call myself a ragdoll
A tattered old thing
With temporary sutures running up my body
They hold my fibers together
Or what is left of them
I look down at my legs
There are holes
I look at my toes
And some have gone missing
I look at my hips
I have a tear
My stuffing is falling out
I move along my body
I gaze at each tragic mark
Counting the times
Reminiscing my life
Before I could even process a thought
I'm grabbed
He plays with me
He throws me
Kicks me
"she's only a ragdoll"
He states
She's not real
But I am
I listen
I smile
I'm there no matter what
But I guess I'm only a ragdoll
My body laying on the ground

cont'd

Bloom.

As my stitching comes undone
My leg slips off
All I can see is the black sky
All I can do is count each star
Because I'm alone again
I open my eyes
I find skin on my legs
It's on my arms
I feel a heart in my chest
And hair on my head
Was it all a dream
I thought it was until I saw his message
Played again
Walking by a store I notice something
My hands reach for a little old doll
"She's a bit of a fixer upper
All she needs is a little love"

- daniela mckillop | *ragdoll*

Massachusetts
https://www.instagram.com/irwin12wow/

long night | quiet drive
bright moon | dark sky
is this how you're supposed to
find out what lifts you

•

creepy street | populated
clouded thoughts | agitated
contentment won't wait for you so
find out what lifts you

•

faded wings | dreaded fears
callused hands | salty tears
you're the only one who can
find out what lifts you

•

big dreams | timid stance
bright smile | one chance
don't let it pass you by
find out what lifts you

- mackalie | *wings*

Nashville, Tennessee
https://www.instagram.com/the.yellow.radio/

<u>part five</u>

THE WIND

POEM WARS

Bloom.

~

THE TAUT remainder of the rope dangled above the boy, just beyond his reach, pulled to the end of its spool. He stretched his arms far above his head, fingers grasping, the frayed end of the rope evading his touch. He stood on his toes, counting the inches, when a deep pain erupted from his ankle and coursed through his body in a reverberant fire, pushing him to his knees, which sank deep into the mud. The flower knelt there beside him in an impassive solitude, staring up at the sky.

Again, the boy stood. The rope lay above him, tempting him, swinging softly in the gloomy twilight.

He took a breath and jumped.

The rope pulled taut and held firm, his hands grasped tightly around the end in a death grip. With a sudden surge of strength, the boy pulled his body upward, locking his legs around the frayed end of the rope. He climbed and climbed, hand over hand, every inch, every foot, the wind whistling louder. His ears filled with the noise, drowning out his pain, drowning out his thoughts.

He was not afraid. There was nothing but the rope and his hands and the wind and the light, which grew louder and closer and brighter with every new handgrip and upward swing.

Then the wind was no longer howling above him, but howling in his ear, and his hands no longer grasped the rope, but grasped the coarseness of wood and stone.

He realized his eyes were closed and he opened them.

Far below was the flower, still caught in the linger of a sunbeam. Then the winds blew, and the clouds gathered overhead, and the sunbeam passed and left the flower in shadow.

Yet the boy knew it was still there.

And, with one final pull, he collapsed on the dry, brittle earth past the edges of the well, the mud and the stones and the flower now far, far away.

Bloom.

Oh, darling, learn to thank the rain.
Let it crash, soak, and pour.
Don't ask it to go away; don't beg it to be tame.
For it is through the storms that you learn:
We need the water to bloom and be more.

- brenna fox | *water me, please*

Orem, Utah
https://www.instagram.com/foxfriendpoetry/

The end is the beginning,
and the beginning is the end.
In between there's confined space where
You & I stand.

See, it's not Love & it's not science,
it's something much more divine.
Something that has been here since the
very beginning of Time.

- pawan | *interstellar*

Raipur, India
https://www.instagram.com/eddytellstales/

Bloom.

I'm somewhere
in between
The beginning
And the end.
I don't know where,
It might be where I'm meant to be
But it doesn't feel right.
I'm fading after every attempt to get up.
I'm a disappointment to my own self
and my loved ones.
Still looking at them in the distance,
my mind has put us apart.

•

Never,
Never say never,
I used to.
I never lie.
I never fail.
I would never do that...
And so it was,
As the addiction wanted me to be.
A fucking liar, worthless piece of shit,
With *failure* stamped on my forehead,
I did, yes.
Again and again,
everywhere.
There was a point I didn't even try to hide.
Isolating myself, or what there was left of me,
Away from any gentle and kind human being who
tried to help me out of that blinding mind of mine.

cont'd

105

POEM WARS

She found me.
Laying almost naked in the middle of the street.
I think I got raped by some drug dealer
on his way to the market.
All I can remember about that night
Among the blur
I saw her golden curly hair,
slightly covering her face.
Her wide open eyes
So brown and clear of fear
I remember her halo; touching me, taking me back
from a place I was willing to go.
From the only place
there's no way back.

•

The next thing I remember
I was at the hospital room,
the nurse was checking on me.
Alone and safe
I was,
alone and safe

•

That was the day I woke up,
opened my eyes
and made my ghosts go away;
forever.

- maría g. | *the awakening*

Murcia, Spain
https://www.instagram.com/feathervspaper/

Bloom.

I was born with the taste of
freedom singing in my heart. Its
mighty power transcribed inside
my bones. The harmonious voices
of wolves howl their praises. In
jade meadows fire flowers whip
about spreading embers to set this
world ablaze. I belong to the wind,
the endless night sky stretching
to the infinity of time. An untamed
garden grows from inside my soul,
all my words coated in wildflower
nectar. I shall find you, and we
shall see each other at long last.
But not yet… not just yet.

- april rose | *someday*

Spokane, Washington
https://www.instagram.com/inspire_imagine0/

time will shatter you.

but it will heal you too.

- hilal hassas | *sabr*

France
https://www.instagram.com/hilal_hassas.writings/

Bloom.

Together we gather at the start;
We stand on the edge of this moment,
waiting for the count down.
faces, unfamiliar and familiar,
young and old, poised to run
into the unknown of a new day.
What dreams do each of us carry?
What hurts will we leave behind,
hoping to out-run their darkness?
Each at his own pace -
each moving to the rhythm
of a story, a song, an unperceived pain.
When the gun is shot -
we find our step, running together,
running alone, toward another year.
My own steps become a prayer,
echoing on winter pavement.
each cold breath a punishment, a gift,
a reminder of this life I have been given.
We all know where we are headed
under this slate sky—to where we first started—
to the finish—to where we first began—
meeting ourselves once again,
trying to comprehend who we were,
who we are,
who we will become.

- mary clare casey | *endings and beginnings*

Cape Cod, Massachusetts

show me death
and I will give life
heavy with meaning-
the kind philosophers
could only dream about

show me fear
and I will give courage
to fall, and to rise
and to fall again,
with grace

show me darkness
and I will give fire
the kind that never burns flesh,
but transcends It.

show me love
and I will return her
beautifully broken
but unscathed by the fictitious
hands of time.

- brett dixon | *seeing*

Boston, Massachusetts

Bloom.

May flowers grow
in your open wounds.

Each time it's picked,
another one blooms.

- saira lakhani | *open wounds*

Toronto, Canada
https://www.instagram.com/poemicium/

i am pulled by the tide of the ocean
to a place unknown
where i'll rage like the stormiest seas
and reflect every light
that the sun shines on me.

i'll be greater than i know.

- katie freddino | *pulled by the tide*

Florida, USA
https://www.instagram.com/katie.freddino.poetry/

Bloom.

cherry blossom
season
comes softly and
all at once a thousand blooms
opening for the rain
that necessary spreading of petals

and that was how
i loved you

- natasha simpson | *cherry blossoms*

Victoria, Canada
https://www.instagram.com/natashaspoetry/

As the tears flowed
I watched each drop
water my pain into
Something beautiful.

- c. johnson | *tears of growth*

United States
https://www.instagram.com/ceeceewriter/

Bloom.

A border that stretches far and wide
Unmarked by gunfight
Bereft of barbed wire and spikes
There are the same people on both the sides
Flying kites in a spotless blue sky
With the freedom to glide as the kites
In a land as undivided as the sky
I'm watching the world through brand new eyes.

Freedom from godmen or freedom from god
Freedom to voice a choice, that freedom is ours
Freedom to worship anyone we like
No caste no race no black no white
No religion is wrong or right
Ram, Allah or Jesus Christ
No more sacrificial lambs, no more sacrifice
I'm watching the world through brand new eyes.

Freedom to birth a girl child
Not killing her before she opens her eyes
Giving her wings to fly and rise
By the freedom to read and the freedom to write
I'm watching the world through brand new eyes.

Freedom to love with one heart, not other minds
Freedom from heteronormative designs
Love at any age, any time

cont'd

Freedom to love of any kind
The freedom to be together, intertwined
Freedom from hate, so free the hostage smiles
I'm watching the world through brand new eyes.

Freedom to dream of a different life
Where one faith unites all of mankind
No flags in the wind, rainbows suffice

Freedom from rich, poor, low and high
They are all alike
The sun shines on, everyone in the spotlight
A slice of heaven, paradise
I watch the world through brand new eyes.

- misha | *freedom*

Delhi, India
https://www.instagram.com/misha.dwivedi/

Bloom.

time to be alone
    build a home out of self
    clean out closets and cravings
    make space
    shed. release.
    space for nothing
    nothing left to chase
    let die
    go dark
    give in to the high
    time to be alone
    savor each breath
    whisper stronger than a yell
    listen
    it's time
    there's a story to tell.

- atlee | *fallen*

Seattle, Washington
https://www.instagram.com/xxatlee/

As her time runs out
I see her sadness return like plagues
I see the storms rage
I see her happiness crash against the rocks
The sun abroad can't keep her
The open air won't need her
She will be isolated
Neglected
She will be lonely and lost
But it is her desire
Because maybe in a place she doesn't belong
She'll find a new identity
But in the place she's returning to
Her identity has already found her

How do you escape yourself
When your shadow is sewn to the ends of your feet?

She has seen the beginning of the beginning
To the end of the end.
And now she is in bloom.

- eli oko | *vacation*

London, UK
https://www.instagram.com/itselioko/

part six

BLOOM

POEM WARS

Bloom.

~

HE DIDN'T know how long he lay there on the ground.

The sand scraped against his cheek, coarse and dry and comforting, the dull ache of his ankle quieted by the whisper of the swaying grass. The boy slowly lifted his face from the sand, eyes closed, and felt the wind. It caressed him with its breath, surrounding him, connecting the earth to the sky.

He opened his eyes.

In front of him drifted a flash of burnt-orange, the flutter of wings. The moth hovered just above the cracked earth, its back warmed by the light, its wings lifted by the air. And then the wind took it, higher and higher toward the sun, and it vanished into the gathering clouds above.

A single drop slid down the boy's cheek. Then another. Then another. He looked up, up toward the sky, eyes clear.

It had begun to rain.

POEM WARS

Acknowledgments

To the soul-baring community of Poem Wars: You have changed me with your words.

To Grammy: Your guidance has helped me navigate the most troubled waters, and has always come at the perfect time.

To Mom: You've nourished me since I was a child in support of my art, and carried me when I could not carry myself.

To Annie: For motivating me to start this project, to never give up, and always follow through ("keep posting!").

To Axel: For showing me that nothing is more important than your dream.

To Atlee: For keeping me on track, organized, and following the path I planned on traveling.

To Bobby B.: Our conversations have kept me in reality, rooted me in sanity, and shown me my values.

And, to Scott: Growing alongside you has given me hope and inspiration on this journey toward self-fulfillment - I couldn't ask for a better friend to travel it with.

About Poem Wars

Poem Wars is an online poetry community, largely based on Instagram, featuring the work of hundreds of poets and followed by over 11,000 people. Its actively growing and highly engaged audience are the contributors that made this book, *Bloom,* turn into a reality.

You can visit the Instagram page via @poem_wars, or visiting the following link:

https://www.instagram.com/poem_wars/

Founded in November, 2017, by R.J. Hendrickson.

About the Editor

R.J. Hendrickson (called Ryan by his friends and family) is a writer and filmmaker, and the founder of *Poem Wars*. His first book, *Follow* - a guide to follower growth-hacking on Instagram - quickly jumped to Amazon's bestseller lists after its publication in the summer of 2018.

A graduate of the University of Southern California's Film and Television Production program, he spent years in the Los Angeles film industry, producing and directing everything from music videos and commercials to feature films. He then moved to Oahu, Hawaii, and worked as a professional photographer before returning to the East Coast, the place of his childhood.

He currently resides in Boston, Massachusetts, and continues to run *Poem Wars*, write, and make films.